SIGNS OF A STRUGGLE

SIGNS OF A STRUGGLE

GUY JAMES WHITWORTH

CLOUDS OF MAGELLAN PRESS | MELBOURNE

This book is for all of Ella's bairns

CONTENTS

FOREWORD

The very first artist I ever met was Guy James Whitworth. We locked eyes when I was a feisty two-year-old, and I was transformed. As his big sister, I took my job very seriously. With a younger brother like mine, that was easy, mind-bending and just downright lovely.

There is a delightful family story about the day my brother was born. Having just welcomed her only son into the world after three girls, our mother, being wheeled along on her hard-earned journey from the delivery ward to the new baby unit, uncharacteristically screamed at the top of her lungs, 'I've had a laddie!' I think she surprised herself as much as the accompanying nurses.

How deeply she fell in love with her new boy on that day and every day.

Northern England at that time, didn't easily birth artists. Boys were still encouraged to adopt male roles in life, careers and personas, yet despite all of that my gentle brother soldiered on and honed his creative skills.

While our childhoods were more often held together by storytelling and family calamities, they also offered endless inspiration and my brother drew it all in, or more accurately, my brother drew it all out! In colour. In black and white. In school sketchbooks and later, in skilful portfolios.

My brother sketches life. As a child, hunched over our dining room table, on the kitchen bench and curled up in his little square bedroom, he sketched. And as he grew older, he sketched in art galleries, pavilions and across all urban life.

On a recent visit to Sydney I attended a life drawing class hosted by my brother. A gothic church acted as a makeshift studio and provided a cool sanctuary on a hot Sydney evening. As my brother gently positioned the nude models, he took care that they were comfortable and confident in their poses, then as the budding life drawing students sipped from glasses of cheap champagne the room inevitably erupted in laughter while my brother helped them configure their best drawing positions and personas!

My brother draws people in and draws out their stories, both told and untold. He laughs at himself and at the world and he eases his models and his viewers. The body of work you see here is just a snapshot, there is so much more, there will always be more, and like my mother before me I want the world to see my brother's artwork. Allow me to shout it out loud.

Dr Dawn Whitworth

Beware of artists. They mix with all classes of society and are therefore most dangerous.

QUEEN VICTORIA

THREE CASUAL DAYWEAR LOOKS

INTRO: THREE CASUAL DAYWEAR LOOKS

 It's not that I don't care what people think, it's more that I've just stopped worrying about it.

Quentin Crisp used to tell a story about standing at a bus stop and how a man wouldn't stop staring. When questioned by the fabulous Mr Crisp on why he wasn't looking away, the man gesticulated towards Quentin's make-up and replied, 'You've got it all on today, haven't you!'

This story always makes me chuckle. I obviously wasn't there in the mid-60s when this particular incident took place, but I have lived this or similar experience so many times.

I've worn make up since my early teens. It started by stealing my older sister's mascara and I pretty much highlighted, concealed, defined and smokey-eyed my way from there on really. Yes, I can go out the house without it, but I rarely ever do. For me to feel confident and complete, then a little highlighter under my eyes, a sweep of blush, lashes of lashes and a couple of say something eyebrows need to be firmly in place.

Mostly I go for a very casual and natural daywear look, but you know, sometimes the devil gets in me and well, who doesn't love a dramatically defined top lip.

So it might come as no surprise that a big part of my creative output is examining masculinity. And by examining, I mean something similar to throwing it in the air and shooting at it. I had an exhibition a few years ago made up of male nudes called What Maketh A Man. It consisted of lots of alternative depictions of possible new masculine ideals. There is, or should be, more to being male than just muscles. I loved exploring this concept, it was an absolute passion project and something I was really obsessive about putting into the world, but fuck, I had to justify and explain it all so many times it was exhausting. Seeing all those willies was nice though.

The way I see the world is different to most people. My idea of masculine probably isn't your idea of masculine. My idea of pretty wouldn't probably be your idea of pretty, and my idea of normal certainly wouldn't be your idea of normal. I'm fine with that and I hope you are too.

I've never really seen aspiring to any level of traditional masculinity as a goal. When looking for partners I've always preferred compassion over cock size (okay, well, look, that's mostly true). I've never really felt particularly male. I dress as male in the same way a drag queen dresses as female. I use stereotypes and fashion clichés to hide behind and convince onlookers. I like being male bodied, I like having a penis – it's fun; and more often than not the men I am sexually attracted to, like that I have a penis too. But you know, or hopefully you know, gender isn't just genitals. An easy way of describing (and labelling) myself is to say I identify as 'gender non-conforming'. I shan't go into that too much here.

A quick trip to Google can sort those 'frequently asked questions' out for you probably clearer than I could, but I will say, as with most things nowadays, gender is on a spectrum and just to make me a moving target, where I sit between feeling male or female is on a sliding scale and woohoo, do I like to slide! Basically gender binaries don't excite or inspire me. Fucking with, distorting and developing them, however, does. I undoubtedly pass as male convincingly enough. Hairy of jaw and deep of voice. Indeed, I do juggle and toy with gender, but very rarely do I feel more female than male. Some gay men would just label me as a 'fem' but I find that very limiting, and certainly more often than not, that term is used in a derogatory way, which just gives me the shits, obviously perpetuating society's bias against women, or belittling the strength of feminine behavioural traits.

I'm a big fan of the term 'gender non-conforming'. I think that kind of works for what I'm trying to say, but doesn't completely sum me up. I still, however, use the pronouns 'he' and 'him'. Why? Because I do, that's why, thank you for asking. I feel that that is right for me and I don't have to make things easy for anyone else to understand. I am me, and I don't have to alter/design/position myself in any other way so it's easier for other people to understand. Understand?

Whenever I apply for grants (that I never get) or fill in surveys I always tick the 'other' box on the form beside gender (or draw one in if required) firstly to make a point but also to add to statistics and shape future societal views, well and fuck with the minds of those in charge of the surveys.

I have a good friend who writes lots about being trans and he often talks about the struggle of transitioning from female to male and about how one of the hardest parts is suddenly being perceived as male by the world, after missing out on a boyhood as a male child in which to practice for being a man. He says he feels short-changed and ill-prepared by life by not having a boyhood. Understandable, and I completely get what he's saying and certainly not to diminish or disregard his experience, but my honest comeback about him missing out on his boyhood is always the same: 'Jeez, love, you'd be welcome to mine!'

To say my childhood was an odd one is a tad of an understatement. Again, I'm fine with that, but that is because I have processed all fuck out of it in my paintings (and I continue to do so), because I either keep swimming with that weight and keep it buoyant, or it will drag me under kicking and gasping for air ('Over dramatic? Me? How dare you!' I scream into the night clutching my pearls and letting my fifteen foot long scarf billow into the wind …)

Anyway blah blah, the following pages are my thoughts and my creations. Pictures and words. Processes and hang-ups. Abilities and embarrassments. The following chapters are about me, you, the people in the paintings and the world we live in. Please do take time to consider and hopefully be at least a little bit inspired by both or either. I'm not saying you'll find many answers but I can guarantee you'll think up a few questions. And, please, do aim those questions at yourself rather than me because what you take from this experience should be more about how you see things than just absorbing how I do.

Think of this as being like sitting next to an eccentric old queen on a long bus journey and he won't stop talking and he keeps showing you pictures on his phone (imagine a combination of me and the fabulous Quentin Crisp perhaps, but please do keep the vision well styled and nothing too 'faded glamour' if you don't mind!). I have a quality bag of lollies and I'm not shy of sharing them. Do however feel free to drift off, look past me out of the window, open a flask, pour yourself a cup of tea and let your mind wander about your own journey as we go …

LIFE ~ PETER DE WAAL

LIFE

When I grow up I want to be Peter De Waal. I've said that a few times to a few different friends over the past few months and it's very true … although I have no immediate plans to actually grow up.

Last year I was really lucky to be offered a job as 'artist in residence' at The Pride in Place conference at Sydney University. It was a conference marking and celebrating the 40th anniversary of the very first Mardi Gras. I was required to sketch some of the original 78ers (and other people of note) who would be present or speaking at the event. It was a dream job and one I instantly accepted. Although to say I was a tad nervous was an understatement, all of these watercolour and pencil sketches were to be executed 'live', as it were. I would be sitting front and centre, just a few feet away from the speakers as they spoke from their podiums, with my sketches clearly visible to the audience behind me. Now, let me tell you, while I like to think of myself as a confident sketcher and certainly not one to buckle under pressure, I am also certainly not fearless or foolhardy enough to avoid accepting that this *could all go horribly, horribly wrong.*

I asked the organisers if I could maybe meet one or two of the speakers before the conference, to get a couple of the sketches out of the way. This was also so I could settle on a particular style and colour palette (yes, I can sketch in a few different styles, it all depends on mood, state of mind and time allowances. Cocky, me? Hell yeah!). I was given two numbers to call, one for someone called (rather intriguingly) Gay Egg (more about that gorgeously inspirational individual another time) and a second called Peter De Waal. Peter's name was vaguely familiar, I was sure I'd read or seen something about him at some point. I spoke with him a few times and shortly after he invited me to his home, Chequerboard, which lead to me knocking on his door with my grubby tote bag of paints and pencils, not really fully understanding what the hell I was doing or what I'd really got myself into.

Peter de Waal is an absolute and utter bloody legend, literally, figuratively and really quite accurately. He has been a human rights activist from before I was born. He was one of the founding members of Australia's *Campaign Against Moral Persecution (CAMP)* and *Phone-a-friend* in the late sixties and seventies. In 1966 he met Peter Bonsall-Boone (aka Bon) who became his partner for the following 50 years, until Bon's passing last year. Scandalously, in 1972 the two Peters shared the first gay kiss ever aired on Australian TV on the ABC's Chequerboard program. Last year he was awarded the Order of Australia for services to the LGBTQI community (as was Bonsall-Boone, although sadly the medal came too late for it to be seen by him).

I knew all of this when I turned up at Peters door all those months ago, after Googling his familiar name, but I'd actually stopped researching after a few brief minutes when I realised how intimidating his achievements were.

You know that feeling when you meet somebody and they greet you and you feel that instant, wonderful, warm, easy feeling of *'we could be friends; I like you'*? Well, that is my overriding memory of what happened when I first met Peter. He is such a naturally warm and lovely man. He has deep set, sparkly eyes and a very easy smile. That someone could be so accomplished, respected and loved yet be so down to earth, practical and unpretentious is an utter wonder of the modern world. He is socially very kind and encouraging; he is a great listener and someone who rarely interrupts (I love people who don't interrupt, because, when I'm really babbling on about nonsense, I really don't want to be stopped).

It is often quite difficult to sketch someone you've only just met and get a very strong likeness. Capturing someone's likeness is also about capturing that person's character. We all guard ourselves socially and often present as someone who we are not to people we don't know. However, with Peter I found him so easy to sketch. So much of what he is about is *being unguarded and open*.

I did four sketches that day. I was actually quite happy with the first one, but I didn't want to leave that quickly. So we sat and chatted, and I sketched, for probably a bit longer than we needed. In hindsight, I do remember him saying he was quite exhausted when I was leaving. I feel quite proud to say, Peter now has one of those sketches framed in his hallway.

I've seen Peter countless times over the past few months at different social events such as rallies. He even invited me, Gay Egg (it really is the *best ever* name) and a few of my mates over to his house for a private showing of the documentary '*Riot*'. The film documents the events surrounding the first Sydney Mardi Gras. That was a pretty special evening, watching 1978 come to life on screen with a couple of the real 78-ers, and hearing all their drama and gossip from 'behind the scenes'.

I really wanted my partner Ryan to meet Peter. A few months ago I took him to see '*Chequerboard*'. I sat and sketched the outside of the house that had seen so much in the last 50 years as Ryan and Peter sat on the front balcony, obviously having a good old gossip about, well, only they know what. I, across the road and unfortunately out of earshot, fended off the neighbours who also offered up their houses for a sketch. I'll be honest:

that special day was slightly marred by my own grumpy jealousy of Ryan's quality time with my new friend!

I like to think Peter De Waal wants to be my friend almost as much as I want to be his and although I do still get a bit intimidated by all his amazing achievements, I just don't allow myself to think about them. And then the intimidation disappears. What really impresses me about him though is that after all his years (he just turned 80) he is never in any way bitter or jaded, but in the face of everything he has seen and done, he is so genuinely humble and lovely. I've said it before and I'll say it again: When I grow up I want to be Peter de Waal!

My only regret is that I missed out on meeting Bon. A few weeks ago I asked Peter if I could use the various sketches I have of him as the basis for a more studied painting. Luckily he agreed; I've been working on the piece since. It is a study not just of Peter, but of Australia's painful and unnecessarily drawn out marriage equality postal vote, along with its process and outcome. It is a piece meant to be melancholic and bitter-sweet with an ever-so-gentle jab to the heart.

Bon passed away only a few months before marriage equality passed into law in Australia and couples of the same sex were finally allowed to marry. This meant this particular couple, who had tirelessly devoted their lives to campaigning for equality and same-sex marriage, were denied that union by timing (and by cancer too I suppose). I'm calling this painting 'Life'.

QUEER JESUS

QUEER JESUS

 I think that title says it all really.

If I am made in god's image then that god is a fabulous, gender nonbinary, same sex attracted and ridiculously stylish individual who can vogue like a motherfucker, apply liquid eyeliner perfectly first go, and nothing you can say can even slightly throw shade on that.

The model for this piece is my friend Bruno again; although I think next time I set out to paint old Jesus fella I think it needs to be with a female bodied model.

Other alternative possible titles for this painting included:

Jesus had 2 dads and he turned out just fine.

The kind of divine being I could kneel before.

Well he did love a flowing robe.

Who doesn't love a seconding coming?

Bless me Daddy, for ooh I have sinned.

AND NOW THAT CAN'T HURT ME ANYMORE

AND NOW THAT CAN'T HURT ME ANYMORE

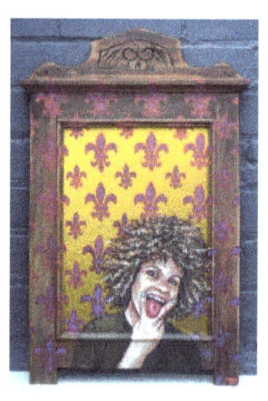

I'd make an utterly rubbish spy. I'm someone who always stands out, whether I want to or not.

I'm fine with that now, but when I was growing up it was a very different story. As an adult I have come to enjoy it and would even say I've managed to make it work for me, but back then, I hated being the centre of attention. I feared it and loathed it. I knew in those instances, it would rarely end well, and did everything I could think of in my early teens to turn down the volume on myself, shrink in size or fade from view.

I knew I wasn't the only one to use these tactics, when I was at school I remember seeing girls around me trying to do the same to avoid the unwanted attention of the school bully-boys. Some girls could deal with and even enjoyed the attention from these boys, but many couldn't.

When you're small, the world around you seems smaller also. For me trying to navigate my way around the twice daily school bus trip to my local High School was particularly stressful and all consuming. The anxiety I experienced hours before each trip was intense. Twice a day I was consumed by this stomach-churning ritual. Once I was trapped on the school bus, anything could happen, I had no escape.

I used to always try to be one of the last to board the bus, that way I'd have to stand, hopefully near the front and close to the calming effect of the bus driver. Whilst it wasn't very enjoyable for the fifteen minute trip, standing/wobbling/leaning into corners, it was far better than having to sit next to someone who was then free to verbally or physically abuse me for the entertainment of others once I was trapped in the seat on that busy bus.

The bullying and abuse I endured for being queer was paralleled only by the randomly explosive sexual abuse the boys on the bus would direct at the girls. If a girl was too confident, she was a slut. If she was too reserved, she was frigid. And so on and so forth, anyone who ever went to any kind of school, anywhere in the world, would know the drill; damned (and demeaned) for what you were and damned (and demeaned) for what you were not.

The route to school was only a couple of miles, although annoyingly just a tad too far to walk and the bus would slowly wind its way through streets and a couple of main roads to get from one place to the other.

The buses in service were a couple of dilapidated old double-decker buses each taking a turn at the twice daily to and fro. In the mornings there was a half past eight pick up, which the popular kids usually went for, because then you got to school at quarter to nine and had that fifteen minutes to hang joyously with your mates, brushing each other's hair, squealing over-excitedly, high fiving or doing whatever popular kids did. The second bus picked up at quarter to nine and would pull up at the school gates with precious minutes to spare before lessons started. This was the one I always aimed for. I certainly wasn't burdened with the worry of meeting friends when I got to school. I was lucky, there were other wayward and bullied kids that I'd sometimes hang out with, but they were casual friendships at best.

There were some kids I connected with but forming real, in-depth connections, was difficult for me because my self-worth took such a consistent battering I honestly didn't understand why anyone would want to be friends with me.

One of the most anxious parts of the ride was that, often certain bus drivers would insist on separating us all, so boys would go upstairs, and girls would have to stay downstairs. This basically just hot-housed the rowdiness to upstairs and condensed my fear of trauma to a point of certainty that I would be abused in some way. As an artist now, scale is something I can confidently say I understand, and it was life experiences such as this, of learning to assess situations and the scale of them, to always minimise myself, that taught me this skill.

There was a particular bridge the bus would always have to drive over. It was an old small bridge that curved slightly on the bend of the road and whenever the boys were upstairs they would do this thing (my anxiety levels still rise just thinking of it) where they would all quickly pile to the side of the bus external to the bend on the bridge with the stomach churning outcome of the bus momentarily leaning outward on 2 wheels and precariously tilting out over the river below. No word of a lie, I would freak the fuck out every time. Talk about a white-knuckle ride! It was awful. Whenever this happened I would also be the only boy left sitting on the other side of the bus, white-knuckling it on my own, as the cheering youths opposite me would hi-five and congratulate each other on, what to me, was an averted outcome of certain death. And there I'd be sitting alone - like I say, I could never be a spy; I could never shrink down quite small enough, easy target, obvious-as-all-fuck-me.

I'm not completely sure of it being connected but, it occurs to me now, I've never been sexually attracted to young men. Give me a nice, wiser daddy type with body hair, the ability to pay for dinner and zero chance of a death wish every time.

Fuck me I really hated those bus journeys.

A strong memory I have is one very horrible school-bus trip where one girl in particular, I can still remember her name, but that's not important here, let's just call her 'Anygirl', because really she could have been, boarded the bus and walked down the centre aisle, all the boys started cheering in a pre-organised routine. She had been seen to hug another girl, on-field during a sporting event, a few days previously and therefore the infinitely wise and all-knowing council of teenage boys had decided she was definitely a lesbian (she was only about 12, so to be honest, she might not have even considered that fully herself at this point). As she boarded and walked down the centre aisle of the bus in perfect unison most of the boys, and some of the girls too, its worth pointing out, all brought two fingers to their mouth, stuck their tongue out in-between and made loud, monstrous moaning noises.

It was awful, and while, on one level relieved to not be the focal point of the attention for once, I know exactly how traumatising that experience would have been for Anygirl. I know undoubtedly that day would have stayed with her and would have shaped the person she became for the rest of her adulthood. I had a similar thing happen to me when once on the bus all the kids decided I was limp wristed and like a vicious-Mexican-wave going along the lines of seats they all started making floppily limp wristed gestures at me and laughing riotously at their own hilarity.

This is a painting of DJ Niveen. I'd met her previously a few times before painting her but didn't really know her that well. When she came around to be sketched we sat on my balcony and gossiped about the people we had in common whilst I nervously drew her for a preliminary sketch.

Originally, in my sketch she had headphones on, but I felt that kind of complicated the final image I wanted. She's very cool but also very real and down to earth and just absolutely lovely. When I tentatively explained what I wanted to do within the finished painting, she was completely up for it straight away.

The 'frame' is something I found in a weekend flea market. It was a part of a broken down vanity unit, there should be a mirror in it, and it would sit atop a table where traditionally a woman would 'prettify' herself. Yeah, bollocks to that! This piece is called 'And now that can't hurt me anymore' and is about processing what I saw on that bus all those years ago. At the time I was so fearful and repressed, I couldn't do anything at all to help Anygirl or deflect the trauma in what was happening. I still internally freeze with fear, and make myself smaller, when I see large gangs of kids in school uniforms; I don't think I will ever not.

I hope this painting is seen by young girls who get this hand/tongue gesture still used against them. I hope when any girls see this painting the gesture depicted becomes something that cannot be used to hurt or harm, but it becomes something in their head similar to a promise for later years, that they will meet women like Niveen and they too will to be charmed by their coolness and relaxed by their down-to-earthiness. I hope that, I really do.

TRUE LOVE

TRUE LOVE

 You know that quote, 'Find a lover who looks at you as if everything you do is magic'? Well, that's certainly one life goal, but for me, another one is just to find a life partner who knows to open a window, unprompted, when they fart in the car.

This is an older painting of mine, a portrait I did of my partner Ryan. Several years ago he and I, but to be honest, mostly him, co-founded a campaign called No Meat May, which, as the catchy title suggests, encourages participants to give up meat, or all animals products, for the month of May. I've always swung between vegetarianism and veganism since the age of nine, and when I first met Ryan he was absolutely everything I would never be looking for in a partner; he was a smoking, (although in the process of quitting) boozing, carnivore. The very first things we agreed on when we met, after chatting a little beforehand online, was that it was for 'no strings attached' sexy, sexy hook-up and that neither of us was looking for a long-term relationship (as we were both each fresh out of one of those).

Well, that was over twelve years ago, and although the clear definition of strings can be a very lose thing, there's a clear argument to say that this big gorgeous fella has me all tied up in the best possible way.

It goes without saying that relationships are hard and always a work in process - compromise and other C words are often called into use. But there is a definite advantage to meeting a partner later on in life, when you both have a few frustrations and failed relationships behind you, to add to the life experience folder, and have a clearer idea of what not to do next time.

I have never really loved anyone the way I do with Ryan, being around him makes me happy. Is it naff to call him my joyfriend? I don't care, I just did. It's a very complete and uncomplicated love. Despite a very (typical of a lot of Australians) real unpretentiousness and often brutal honesty, he still somehow manages to fill me with both awe and creative inspiration. Sometimes I find myself looking at him as if he's magic, although, just to keep it real, that's not to say I don't still scream at him to open a window when he farts in the car and hope he can just get away with it, or not want to sometimes pull a pillow lovingly over his face and press down firmly when he wakes me up with his snoring.

Back when we first met, I remember clearly sitting opposite him, coughing slightly in the smoking corner of the pub we sat in, and thought; yeah, this one could be dangerous. Not because he gave off any sort of clichéd 'bad boy' vibe, but because of the exact opposite; he really didn't. Okay, embarrassing kinky admission coming up; I have a very particular fetish: I am an absolute slut for compassionate men. Just to be really graphic here, I'm talking the kind of man that can do some random act of kindness without needing even the slightest recognition for it. The kind of person who will put aside years of ingrained macho bullshit to emotionally give, without shame or bravado, without even realising the revolution that act contains. I've never been drawn to the moody and self-destructive type, (urrgh), I have enough of a gaping emotional wound of my own I'm trying to tend to, thank you. Give me a man who wants to nurture, encourage and enable the underdog and my tighty-whitey's drop every time! But that is not to say I don't also try my best to supply those things when it's my turn; again, I've enough life experiences to know when it's not my turn with the talking stick, it isn't all about me and when I'm just background support crew.

There is a theory, that all oppression is linked. The kind of person who can justify racism can without doubt also justify homophobia, or sexism, or ableism or, well, look, the list goes on. When I met Ryan he ate meat and that was problematic to me, but pretty much everyone I knew at that time ate meat, and that was a compromise to my beliefs that I had made constantly in all sorts of relationships; but over the next few years, Ryan, without much encouragement from me, ate less and less animal products until deciding to ultimately go vegan. His path to that decision was different from mine, but it was a very nearby destination and neither of us now eat any animal products (meat, milk, eggs, etc.) at all. The reason I mention the 'all oppression is linked' thing is because to me 'speciesism' is the next on the list of prejudices from above. I believe anyone who can remotely devalue life, any life, of any living creature, can also within the same mindset unconsciously devalue another set of beings when it becomes convenient or necessary. Basically we all have it in us to fart in the car and hope we can get away with it. Unfortunately, with the consumption of meat and the impact that factory farming has on the already at-crisis-point environment, none of us can get away with it. Extreme vegan farts are pretty unbearable, yes, I'll give you that, but extreme weather conditions and the end of human existence as we know it doesn't really give us a lot of other options.

I am so lucky that I have a life partner who shares my views, and even better than that, wants to make a change in the world for the better. Relationships are hard but changing the world is harder. It's a bold and brave thing to attempt. No Meat May might not exactly save the world, but it's a gateway project that certainly helps towards it. I painted Ryan quite small in the painting because that's often how he seems: small to the world and slightly misplaced in it. But that world within the painting is still bright, loving, warm pink and optimistic.

Relationships are hard, but less doomed if you are prepared to evolve. Sometimes that's hard work, but to save the relationship it's necessary. As I see it, to save the environment, halt global warming and save ourselves, humankind simply has to evolve. There is no global window to wind down and apologies aren't going to cut it. Magic doesn't exist. Go vegan, because if you are going to fart you might as well make it a fucking spectacular one.

FREEDOM IN THE SHADOWS

FREEDOM IN THE SHADOWS

I first got into the bike paintings because I needed something to do in my studio when there was no one around to paint. I certainly don't struggle with a lack of wonderful people around me to inspire me, but life happens, and I'm often left at the mercy of people's availability or even anxiety levels when it comes to convincing them to model for me. So sometimes it's useful to have a fall-back to work on during the days when a model is a no-show. Oh the countless masterpieces I could have painted if it hadn't been for the models texting me on the day telling me about how their earlobes have exploded, or some other similarly convincing tale on why they can't make it …

My vague fascination with, and appreciation for bikes started when I was younger, when bikes were both a mode of independent transport and a means of escape. I talk easily about the bullying I endured as a child, and while processing that is an ongoing theme in my work, in balance, whist much of my childhood was dysfunctional, it was also in contradiction, still sometimes very loving. As much as most of it was a struggle, some of it, albeit often fleetingly, was idyllic and even ideal. I have a sister who is two years older and we really were the best of friends growing up. If it hadn't been for her, I actually doubt I would have made it. Whilst we definitely need more women in power in this world, as a lesser alternative, if only every man who ever got into a position of power had had the joys of a sister just slightly older to show him how the world could work. Older sisters undoubtedly make very good friends and role models to young men.

Together my sister and I would embark on, what seemed at the time, incredibly far reaching bike rides and those days are blissful memories. Where I grew up in Northumberland, on the North East coast of England, we were not far from the Scottish borders, and that sometimes bleak yet sometimes beautiful countryside that I had as my playground is some of the most striking in the world. I was the youngest of four children and as is often the case with the last child, my parents allowed me a lot of freedom, not that I was always confident enough to take it, but as the only boy child it was presumed I could look after myself, and mostly I did.

A few years ago, when I took my partner back to Northumberland to meet the family, he was completely blown away by the landscape. There are, literally, medieval castles at every turn and the rolling hills and meadows in the summertime are picture postcard perfect. Unfortunately, the area is just as homophobic as it is picturesque, so swings and roundabouts and punches to the face there I suppose. That last sentence still in mind, it'll come as no surprise that I moved to London (the minute I could) at eighteen. Whilst I was happy to make the move and I always knew I would never be moving back, initially living in London wasn't the dream I was hoping for and a fair few times, after dropping out of Fashion College, I found myself penniless and sometimes even homeless on those unforgiving streets. It was as much through necessity as it was through design that I once again got on my bike, so to speak, and continued that life-long love affair with my two wheeled trusty steed.

Looking back on my days cycling around that big scary capital city I'm amazed at my own freedom and fearlessness. I would cycle unfazed through the blaring horns and reckless drivers of Marble Arch and Piccadilly, I'd cruise casually to (dodgy) jobs life-modelling at Art Schools in Chelsea and effortlessly sail over bridges to late night rendezvous with (equally dodgy) men north of the river Thames. Ah yeah, them were the glory days …

However, my current infatuation with bikes isn't as practical or heart-healthy as that, now my journeys with them is almost purely an inspirational trip. I do still own a bike and I do head out on the occasional bike ride, but my love affair has now morphed into a salacious objectification of the bicycles form. What inspires me now with bikes is their limitless potential; to me they represent the essence of freedom. As I edit this chapter for print I am in Berlin attending a conference where Ryan is giving a couple of talks about No Meat May and we have hired bikes and are cycling around and exploring this awesome and creative city. In a world where freedom, either personal and/or political can be so easily taken for granted, I think bikes serve as a perfect metaphor to remind us of both, how easily that freedom can be taken away and also of just how much that freedom exists if we choose to take advantage of it. I have entitled this ongoing series of bikes 'Freedom if you want it' which (if you could please just ignore the knowing nod to John and Yoko for the moment) is rather self-explanatory. I never paint locks on the bikes I depict, they lie, stand or lean there ready to be taken by whoever is brave or needy enough.

On a personal level, the freedom of my youth, the escape of my youth, the independence of my youth and the men of my youth, all await me when I picture the places those bikes could whisk me away to. But then on another level our personal freedoms are constantly being eroded by politicians on all sides around us, workers' rights, women's rights, allowances for religious freedom to name a few examples, all impact on choices made available to us and how we live, whether we are aware of it or not.

When I was living in London in the mid-eighties, there was a slogan used on posters to alert (or purposefully alarm) people to the perils of HIV and AIDS; 'Don't die of ignorance'. Well, while I'm not sure of how effective that poster campaign was, certainly the people I saw struggling with HIV-related illnesses didn't find themselves in those situations solely through ignorance, I do think those words are indeed still good advice. We need to be aware of the world we live in, and sometimes we need to be reminded that if left to its own devices society may not always peddle in the right direction, or brake fast enough.

As I've worked my way through this series of bike paintings, the way I've come to regard the bicycle paintings has changed, at first I saw what I was depicting as either a still life or a landscape of sorts, but now I see each painting as more of a portrait. Capturing the unique personality, the potential and well-being of each bicycle is as important as its surroundings.

I understand completely the stress and worry of stepping forward to be an artist's model, exploding earlobes or disappearing legs or absolutely any ailment can strike on the day in question. I thoroughly understand peoples' fear of the unfamiliar, how brave people must be to actually follow through and turn up when they do. Not everyone would offer themselves to be stared at, interpreted and envisaged in bright garish colours and reduced to a representation of a sexual cliché.

So with that in mind, joyously once again, it appears, bicycles have saved me and offered an escape from the frustrations of life. Freedom always exists, even if it is sometimes hidden amongst the shadows.

RED HAIR AND THE ORANGE CHAIR

RED HAIR AND THE ORANGE CHAIR

This is one of my favorite paintings.

I started painting it the day after hearing from an old friend that they had been diagnosed with cancer. This friend was known for her shock of short, bright red hair and when she called me to tell me of her diagnosis the only time her voice wavered and struggled was at the bit about going through chemotherapy and being in the process of losing that hair she was known for.

Gawd bless her. She is one of those tough, 'I'd much rather have you by my side in a fight than against me' types, I certainly wouldn't want to mess with her, ooh she's a formidable one, although that said, she is also an absolute sweetie who is as soft and warm as anything if she likes you. In Australia there's an expression, 'they're a good sort', and she really, really is.

Anyway the day after we chatted I was feeling really down, although my friend sounded like she was definitely on the road to recovery, cancer had already taken both of my parents and a plethora (love that word) of other wonderful people over the years and my friend's news just kind of reignited some of that darkness and grief. It was a dull, cloudy old day and I was walking vaguely through the streets of Surry Hills thinking all of this through, with the weight of it all beginning to pull me down.

However I looked up and saw this spectacular bright orange chair. Just standing alone, slightly oddly outside a cafe, all on its own, regardless of the weather. It just looked like it was so happily shiny through all of life's bullshit. Bright orange but with a deep long shadow doing its best to crack it in two. And then, as if by magic, just to add another beautiful layer of wonderment, while I was staring at it, the sun came out and bathed it in the most delicious, dancing, dappled light and I honestly wanted to cry with the perfection and beauty of the thing.

You know what I was forced to re-recognize that day? (because, yeah, I know we all already know this) Life is for living! It's such a dumb-fuck-nonsensical cliché I know, but it is completely true. Live your life. If you have no interest in painting the chair then at least look for the chair. Fight to see the chair if the view is obscured. Battle the fucking cancer and make every day count towards the grand sum of your life. And absolutely grow your hair back too, if you think it defines you, but don't let that shit rule you. I started to lose my hair at 16 and although it was pretty darn depressing at the time, ooh I've had a lot of sex over the years because some men believe bald is beautiful.

Anyway I painted the chair so you don't have to.

I sent a copy to my friend and told her about it and I think she thought I was a bit mad and a bit over-dramatic and she might well be right, but fuck it, because, you know, whatever gets you through, right?

SELF-PORTRAIT AS MARDI GRAS

OR CAN THE PERFECT WIG COVER FORTY YEARS OF OPPRESSION?

SELF-PORTRAIT AS MARDI GRAS

OR CAN THE PERFECT WIG COVER FORTY YEARS OF OPPRESSION?

 Self-portraits are hard. You have to sit facing yourself in a mirror and work out what's real and what's hoped for, or what's projected.

I know my limitations, I already know my flaws, my faults and my fuck ups! I don't want to sit staring at them until my brain hurts. My top lip is too thin. My jaw too soft. My head too bald. My nose too wonky.

Yet here I am. Yet here I am. Full frontal, face on and flabby.

Some days I like who I am and what I can do; most days I don't like what I look like.

I like what I am from the inside looking out but not from the outside looking in.

I look like my mum and my dad combined; I look like the worst bit of him and the best bits of her. Her - kind, warm, funny and accepting. Him - fierce, angry, unpredictable and cold. I am in-between gender, in-between ever fully knowing either, made of him and her, made of fragile light and relentless darkness and hope and anger and love and hate and fear and fearlessness. Here I am.

The wig is hot and itchy, my back is cold and the light keeps changing. I'm a forty *cough* something year old man sitting shirtless in a room looking at himself in a cheap nylon wig trying to connect with something I hope I am, but fear I am not, and unable to objectively externalise or realise either.

So it turns out men's tits sag too as they get older.

I see my limitations, but I try to embrace them as something I have worked on and achieved success with. I am (roughly) the same age as Sydney's Mardi Gras and I am just as fucking fabulous.

I am a parade.

I am glitter, I am pink, I am rainbows, I am strength, I am loud, I am a riot, I am bright lights on dark nights, I am bags under my eyes, I am a quick finger bang in a toilet queue, I am a fumbled blow-job behind a truck, I am kicked to the ground by authorities, I am fearless and fucked and I am everything I can make myself into if I choose and I choose to be this.

Although I don't really.

He made me. She made me. Society made me. The state made me. All I did was add the sparkle to cover the bruise.

I am a well-trodden parade route. Nothing new, nothing to see, nothing to applaud but the idea of spectacle and the disappointment of a few tawdry sun-bleached sequins. Shake them baby, shake them. Yet here I am and still I strut. Still I twirl, middle finger in the air, defiant and purposeful.

I am pointed at by tourists, I am laughed at by straights, I am formed by the corporate dollar and I sometimes lose track of where I came from. And I feel myself changing into something I shouldn't be, shaped by people who care nothing for what I could truly become.

Yet here I am. Full frontal, facing forward, just keep marching, not fearless but forcing myself forward anyway.

Fuck them. Paint me.

This is who I am and if I can bare to face myself in such a harsh light then I can learn to love myself in a softer one with the benefit of a rosy yet accurate recollection of what brought me here.

I'm not perfect but I am all I have.

Can the perfect wig cover 40 years of oppression? No fucking idea, but the thing about these cheap wigs is that they always bounce back into shape and mostly so do I.

THE LIGHT THAT SHINES OUT OF MARIA

THE LIGHT THAT SHINES OUT OF MARIA

Can a comedy moustache save the world? Look, I doubt it, but it did at least save this painting from being painted over.

I have mixed emotions on this piece. I painted it a few years ago and loved it when I painted it. The sitter's name is Maria, and you know that thing when you meet someone and you are just blown away by their positive energy and, as is often the case with me, you want to be their friend, but you don't really think you're interesting or funny/clever/special enough, but you really try to be their friend anyway because you really want this person in your life and then that, in turn, kind of makes you strive to be a better person? Maybe that is just a 'me thing'. I don't know, but anyway, I was so super-impressed by Maria that I decided to try and capture that radiant awesomeness in a painting. It's worth pointing out I had just had an exhibition of male nudes, so was also thinking about balancing out my portfolio by including more female nudes, a naïve thought process I know; but it kind of made sense at the time.

Obviously, I know about the objectification of women, the politicising of the female nude and of course, as I mention elsewhere, I purposely try to avoid the exploitation of anyone in my work. Bearing these things in mind, when I originally set out to paint the picture, I intended Maria to wear a faux leather harness (leather master style), a big comedy moustache, stick on bushy eyebrows or maybe some dorky 50s-style wing-tipped glasses and we talked about incorporating these and a few other options to de-sexualise the piece. But when I got towards finishing the painting, maybe it was vanity, maybe it was laziness, maybe it was that old foe of mine 'wanting to fit in', I don't know, but I decided the piece looked fine and complete without any of those 'gimmicks' and left it as a straight up portrait/nude.

My opinion of the painting, which up until this point I was quite proud of, changed when I put it into an exhibition (called rather subtly Artist, Activist, Arsehole) and people started to share with me what they thought about it.

Well, so yeah, you can guess the rest, the portrait got attention for reasons I wasn't really happy with and there was certainly no way that this image of Maria wasn't being sexualised by the straight men (and for that matter some of the lesbians) who viewed it.

It was completely my fault, and it was a trap that I had stupidly wandered directly into, as I'm sure many painters had before me. Thankfully the painting didn't sell at exhibition and when I got it back home, I had this weird feeling which I can only describe as being slightly ashamed of it, and rather tellingly stacked it away behind a few other paintings in my studio. I had failed in what I had set out to do. But, you know, how can you know success without firstly knowing failure? Fine, I thought, learn a lesson, move on, forget about it.

It took me a couple of years to think about the painting again without the shame of failure. I liked the piece and I liked what I had set out to say with it. Sure I had been naive, but my intentions were honest, so I contacted Maria and checked she was cool with my plan and sat down once again with the piece on my easel and painted the glorious moustache that you now see before you. Long story short; I got a bit carried away and added a beard for good measure. In for a penny, in for a pound! I definitely should have done it earlier, but better late than never. I suppose the lessons learnt are: always trust your gut instincts, don't be afraid to follow through when you know deep down you are right, and don't worry about other people's opinions.

Once again, I am now happy with the piece. It finally says what I want it to, it still is a portrait of someone of incredible physical beauty and energy but, there is no chance of it being read as something I didn't intend it to be. It reminds me of the Laughing Cavalier by Frans Hals, but a gender-fuck version. It's a funny old world we live in. Look, I don't think a moustache can save the world but if it can reduce the sexual objectification of women then it'll go some way towards helping.

RESPECT YOUR QUEER ELDERS

RESPECT YOUR QUEER ELDERS

 One of my first ever jobs was working in a gay pub in Soho, in London back in the late eighties. OMG, I loved it, I was eighteen, ludicrously dumb, ridiculously naïve (although I didn't think so at the time) the cutest I've ever been (all relative), worryingly slim (again, despite what I thought at the time) and I got to flirt and fiddle with some quite delicious men.

I really did have the most fun ever. I would leave the house to start my weekly shifts on a Wednesday and I often wouldn't get home till Monday night to sleep my 'weekend' away. After shifts, I would often go home with customers from the pub or go clubbing after work and end up just going straight back to work the next day (I'd buy a cheap t-shirt and have a full body wash down in the women's toilets, just in case you were wondering about the hygiene involved in such a lifestyle choice)

Unfortunately, I wasn't the only presence making itself known on the gay scene at the time, there was a new disease that had been known as GRID (gay-related immune deficiency) but had recently become re-christened as AIDS.

It was a dark and scary time. A lot of people around me were being diagnosed as HIV+ and the gay world was effectively in shock, unable to process fully what was happening. Information was scattered and often contradictory, it felt like no-one really knew what caused or spread the disease. I slept around a fair bit, but always kept to what was vaguely then called 'safer sex' although my boundaries around what that was exactly were very dependent on the moment, and often (stupidly) how much I liked the person I was having sex with.

It was also a frustrating and angry time, well for me anyway. I was angry at a lot of things and I joined a queer activist group called Outrage. We went on lots of shouty demonstrations and campaigned for clearer information around HIV/AIDS and for more effective treatments. In that group there was a filmmaker/artist I really admired called Derek Jarman. Typically, I never could muster up enough courage to talk to him; he was everything I wanted to be and wanted in a man. He was brave, unique, a creative genius, and never tried to hide his sexuality, and then in later years, his HIV status. He once smiled across a crowded room at me and it was like my self-worth instantly tripled, it was like being caught in a surprise sunburst on a cloudy day. He had seen me. I existed.

I volunteered at a charity called The Terrence Higgins Trust and became a 'Buddy' - a person allocated to support and assist someone who was struggling with fully blown AIDS and needed a friend to lean on. A lot of people I knew from those days of support groups and memorials aren't around anymore. I remember once standing sobbing alone in a charity shop on Fulham Road. I had to go to my friend's funeral, I couldn't find a black jacket to fit me and all the sleeves on all the jackets were too long and I didn't have the money, or time, to have them taken up. I really lost it in that changing room, I can only imagine what I must have sounded like from outside. Short arms and limited funds can be extra curses to those struggling with monumental grief.

It was around this time that my friend (Beverly, she looked a bit like supermodel Linda Evangelista but a jolly, Scottish version who swore lots and lived off bags of crisps) lent me her oil paints, bought me a canvas and none too subtly suggested I work through some of the emotional baggage I was beginning to carry.

Skip to a few decades later and late last year I got a job leading a few 'Art workshops' for a Queer youth group a few suburbs away from where I live here in Sydney.

The booking was for four Thursday evenings for the month before Christmas and I ambitiously pitched running the groups as sessions all based around identity, specifically Queer Identity, and what that could mean using portraiture as a medium of self-expression.

The young people were all street-smart teenagers somewhere on the LGBTQI spectrum and the afternoon before the very first class, I had the very nearest thing approaching a panic attack I've ever experienced in my life. What if those sassy young queer people hated me? What if they all ganged together and started bullying me? The group was held in a youth centre in a very working class suburb of Sydney, what if I came across as too posh and too privileged and the kids couldn't relate to me? What if, what if, what if?

Anyway, of course, each session was awesome, I absolutely loved the experience. It was so inspiring, informative and utterly life affirming. The future is here and it is queer. The ridiculously over-thought-through-theme of identity was soon abandoned, as it became clear, that the best possible outcome was that these young people just got to experience a chilled out, safe, creative and queer space where nothing was expected from them other than for them to do their own thing and explore being creative.

It was a complex feeling when it struck me, like a big pink queer steam-train full of rainbow flags, while in the second session, that the couple of social workers who had arranged this booking had done so, not because I was clever, arty or pretty, but because I was actually an older queer person, and that had been the real intention of those social workers all along. The group sessions were really about introducing the younger people present to someone who was older and completely comfortable with themselves their creativity and their queer sexuality.

I was so lucky that I got to London when I did; I had many older, queerer and more sorted people I got to look up to, whose smile and attention could give my self-worth such a boost and encourage me to know I existed. I got to live among and share experiences with elders, before the AIDS crisis in the nineties really kicked in, I got to experience a glorious mass of all ages of queers, as yet untouched by the decimation that was to come in the following decades.

The LGBTQI communities are missing a lot of people who did not get to make it through to get their stories told, their frustrations shared and their life lessons learnt from. There are gaps and missing pieces in our social jigsaw that were taken from us. We are all poorer because of that.

The painting above is called 'Respect Your Queer Elders' and is mainly made up of 3 primary colours, red, yellow and blue. These are the essential 3 colours that all other colours come from. Just like the equality that is now almost in our grasp, everything that the LGBTQI communities are currently experiencing, has come from those people who have struggled, fucked, campaigned, shouted and protested before us. The models for this piece are Michelle Frances Collocott and William Yang, both elders who have earned their place of respect in the creative queer community.

I don't completely consider myself as a queer elder yet, although realistically I'm not far off it; however I do consider myself one of the lucky ones who gets the chance to enjoy that privilege.

AUSSIE JESUS

AUSSIE JESUS

 I moved to Sydney from London when I was 28. I was ready to move, London had been good to me, but it was too big, too busy, too distracting, and I was too easily distracted.

I'd had a few little exhibitions and was beginning to work out what I wanted to say with my artwork, but it was all still a bit half-thought-through. I wanted time to concentrate more on my art practice and I knew London wouldn't give me the peace and quiet needed to do that. My Australian boyfriend at the time, who was gloriously tall, ridiculously handsome and as dumb as a bag of hair, asked if I wanted to come back to Sydney with him and start a new life with him there. We had been together two years and it was as close to true love as I was capable. For the sake of this memoir let's call him Tim, not his real name, firstly because I'm kind, and secondly, because I don't want to get sued. Anyway, I thought about nice but dim Tim's request for about 3 seconds and jumped into his arms and said yes. Let's be honest, like attracts like.

Deep down I knew Tim wasn't 'the one' but he was the closest I'd ever been to that at that point. He was a simple soul who didn't like anything 'too weird' or creative and I definitely knocked the corners off myself to fit the mould of the boyfriend he was looking for, and I think we can all agree that is never a good thing. But, the move to Australia looked like it could be a loved up, sex filled adventure with a really good looking man, and what was the worst that could happen, right?

It took just over a year for my visa to come through … well, that wasn't the best year of my life, I have to say, limbo can be a delightfully entertaining dance move but not an enjoyable state to live in. Eventually after jumping through many hoops and acquiring certified copies of every document known to humankind, I convinced the Australian consulate that Tim and I were meant to be forever together for never to part, the visa was stamped into my passport, and off I flew; dumb, niave and without a worry in the world.

I remember the joy of running through that Arrivals hall at Sydney airport, my life was complete, I'd finally made it to Tim, he and I were in love and the world (or at least the as-of-yet undiscovered southern hemisphere) was a wonderful place! We hadn't seen each other for almost a whole year, and I had been faithfully (well, mostly) waiting for this very instant. This was my rom-com special once-in-a-lifetime-moment as I ran into his arms. It's worth pointing out this was in the days before internet, so the only contact had been really quick and expensive phone calls and vague and uninformative but sexy/ generically loving postcards, so to say we hadn't been in close contact in the past year was an understatement. Anyway, short story even shorter, by the time we had left the airport in what turned out to be his new boyfriend's car, the relationship was over and I didn't know another single living soul on this side of the planet. Nice one Guy, well played.

Even by my standards (and I wasn't exactly known for having standards) this relocating for love thing hadn't been my wisest move. It's also worth pointing out, in hindsight, this wasn't really Tim's fault either; I hadn't fallen in love with him for his faithfulness and emotional intelligence, and you know, bless him, he'd been working with the tools he'd had to hand. Relocating back to Australia and managing a long-distance relationship had proved too much for him to handle and, really, on some level, I'd known that it would be. Tall and handsome Tim, I have no idea where you are in the world now, so I hope you're happy (Oh please, who am I kidding, I stalk that motherfucker on social media on a regular basis and I know his every move to this day and by the look of things he's still as dumb as a bag of hair, although that's the only hair he has left and let me tell you; I was the best thing that never happened to him!) and of course I wish him all the best.

After a few days of licking my wounds (and causing as much trouble as I possibly could in Tim's new relationship) I pulled myself together and set about calling Australia home. I had nothing to stay for, but also little to go back to. In hindsight, people get through worse, but at the time it was a bit of a struggle. I found a job working in a clothes store in Darlinghurst and found an apartment with another single gay guy who ended up being a really good friend, I shall call him Marc because that's his name, and that fucker wouldn't dare try and sue me, because he knows I know all the quality filth on him and I'd be more than happy to air some of those stories in a court of law, let me tell you!

(I remember late one night Marc and I went out together to the local gay bar, The Albury, for those who care, and we both went out wearing tight white t-shirts and purposefully stood out in the pouring rain for a good 5 minutes before we walked in, throwing those doors wide open so every man in the place checked us out! Who knew white t-shirts go practically see-through when wet! Well, we both did, obviously. Kindred slutty spirits.)

I've now been in Australia for just over 20 years, although with a few brief international adventures and years away in between. It was a bumpy start, but I never found any reason to not want to be here. I never really wanted to come here before being asked and I never thought I would spend as long as I have, but hey, here I am! Yes, summers are too hot and winters are too cold, but that's what air-con and cardigans are for. Yes, there are too many killy things that live here like spiders and snakes and sharks and so on, but I don't bother with them much and so far none of those creatures has really bothered with me. There are good things about living here there are bad things about living here. Vegemite is good, the relentless oppression of Indigenous people and the lack of recognition around the country being founded on genocide is really very bad.

Artistically I would say I still feel equally as inspired by European backgrounds as I do by my still newish Australian surroundings, but that ebbs and flows with how I'm feeling. I love the lack of pretention here and I love the fact that the national identity of the land is still forming (and formable). It unsettles me how much Americana is worshipped and emulated in politics and pop culture. I feel sick at how indigenous Australians are treated and I try to be part of the halting of colonisation rather than being yet another immigrant insisting their culture is the best culture. Treading that line between encouraging influences and avoiding cultural appropriation is difficult, but worth the effort and outcome. I have painted a few indigenous people that I've met along my way, but I haven't included those paintings here, I feel I must be careful of exploiting those that have already been hideously exploited. Theirs is not my tale to tell or claim as my own. I once met an aboriginal man who simply refused to talk to me and I completely understand why, if I was him, I'd want to punch me for what I represent and from the corrupt systems I (may not be solely responsible for, but undoubtedly still) benefit from.

This painting is me processing my Australianness and Australian-isms. Although that said, I'm first to admit that my identity around my citizenship is still free forming in my head. Australia, funny place with a funny name, funny people and sometimes not-very-funny-at-all politics.

Twenty years on and I'm still waiting for that rom-com ending moment where it all makes sense. I mean it mostly makes sense now, but not all. I still have more questions than answers about what I'm trying to do with my life and what I'm attempting to say with my art. I miss out on lots of grants and residencies because I admit to my European background and influences way too easily and according to some (*everyone* is an art critic) I can't be considered a great Australian artist because I haven't assimilated completely enough. Did I even try, mostly, I don't know. Not a lot of what I'm doing or am expected to do makes sense, I don't always understand life, maybe it was me that was as dumb as the bag of hair all along?

I often wonder what would be different in my world if it had all gone well with Tim and I continued to knock corners and edges off myself. I don't think I would be painting as much, indeed, if at all. I doubt I would have pushed myself that hard. I am pretty sure I wouldn't be as surrounded by the alternative queers I now call my peeps, they would have been much too progressive for Tim. Bruno, the beautiful model in this painting, is a non-gender conforming fem identifying individual who I couldn't imagine ever even meeting while I was with Tim, they are such worlds apart in their lifestyles and life choices. All this said, Tim actually never really was a bad person; he just made a few choices that didn't benefit me and as with many ex's we all vilify that because it's easier than seeing it all from their perspective and realising we too are to blame for the relationship failure.

This painting, Aussie Jesus, is about gender, rejection and the 'not being good enough' that religion pushes onto us. But it is also about acceptance for who we are, feeling accepted, comfortable and complete in the culture that surrounds us. It is about not having to knock edges off yourself to fit in or feel loved. Be who you truly are and you will ultimately find friends who will stand out in the rain with you until your t shirt is suitably see through. The struggles I faced for my first few months all alone in Australia definitely would have shaped me, but they never came close to breaking me. Would I still be the person I am now; would my creative output still have the same things to say if things had gone more to plan? Who knows, I think probably not if I was with Tim, but I'm here now and I'm happy and I'm painting and that was definitely worth making the trip for.

ALL THE FEELINGS THE DAY AFTER THE ELECTION
RESULTS

ALL THE FEELINGS THE DAY AFTER THE ELECTION RESULTS

 I think the title of this piece speaks for itself. Modern (world and local) politics just frustrate me so much.

I spent a lot of my earlier life struggling with depression. I totally get the concept of likening depression to the image of the black dog who walks along beside us when we are encircled by those thoughts of despair. I have had days, weeks and months in the past of dwelling in those places of hopelessness und unproductiveness. I have totally had days where that dog sits on my chest and stares into my eyes, the vile dribbling foul breathed beast. It can suggest things, hurtful, self-harming, miserable things. But I actively now try to structure my life so those feelings don't get to be made welcome. I have never been one of those artists that is at their most productive when using negative experiences as their starting point.

Ah, now hold on there, you may say, what the fuck, Guy, you use your frustrations with the world constantly as a reference point! You big nonsensical homosexual hypocrite you! (honestly, do you mind, there's no need to be so aggressive!) However, no, you're only a bit right, I do process negative thoughts and events, but my starting point for most of my work is an intent to create something bright and colourful and uplifting, once that is imagined, only then will I dip into, and process the frustration needed to create the piece. That way I know whatever I'm working on won't overwhelm or disempower me (or beckon over the stinky, snarling black dog). Does that make sense?

I always try to use humour, colour, process, light, optimism and strength to form my art. I also try my best to let these things shape my life. Nowadays I very rarely allow thoughts that encourage the black dog to walks alongside me, I do however welcome a multi-coloured zebra called Barbra and right now I'm training that glorious motherfucker to jump through hoops, mix the perfect G & T and do the cha-cha and if the art-buying public doesn't quite get that, then I hope their own black dog bites them on the arse, or not, because me and Barbra the zebra have got places to be and people to do.

THE KING AND QUEEN OF THE REVOLUTIONARY SCENE

THE KING AND QUEEN OF THE REVOLUTIONARY SCENE

Over the past year or so I've really grown tired of the expression 'living my best life.' It's one of those sound bites that, although marvellous in its intent, doesn't always really say anything at all, and it's become quite omnipresent on reality TV shows and online media. It's become the kind of thing toothy American teenagers say on their YouTube channel while spouting some dodgy life advice often from the point of preposterous privilege. Yet, last month when I sat in the crowd at the memorial held for Candy Royalle that very expression went through my head. Candy without doubt, with great effort and focus, had absolutely lived her best, albeit too brief life.

This is the oldest painting I'm including here, it is a painting in an older style, of Candy and drag performer Dallas Dellaforce.

In the months since Candy's passing there have been many words written, spoken and sobbed and it is justified to say that she leaves behind both an impressive legacy and ongoing inspiration from her life and work. Although still successful in describing the public persona of someone I was lucky enough to call a good friend, I feel few of these many eulogies really summarised Candy in a way I would recognise.

Candy and I always had a strange, hard to define friendship, where I often struggled to know if she ever deep-down really liked me or just tolerated me as being a part of her tight, fabulous, queer and creative social group. We would often have disagreements, I remember a particularly glorious one a few years ago during a concert in Sydney on a scorching hot Australia Day (we were seeing Florence and the Machine, I really am a fan!) and Candy and I spent a lot of that concert angrily shouting over the music about whether the flags of all nations should be abolished! I believed no, Candy believed yes. Years later, I still have my belief, but I understand her points more.

The first time I sketched her it was for an exhibition of nudes and she was massively offended that when she offered to remove her bra I turned her down; I only wanted an upper shoulder portrait. We discussed the (to me quite comical) disappointment she felt, much later, when she accused me of being afraid of women's bodies. I have thought about this many times since. Yes, she wasn't wrong, women's bodies and sexuality do unnerve me a little and she definitely picked it (I've worked on that a lot in the many years since, but still with more work to be done).

I have a small faded piece of paper carrying a handwritten poem from Candy on my fridge, she gave it in a thank you card to my partner and I after we dropped off food while she was going through her first round of chemo. Out of the few dishes we dropped off she liked my curry pasties best (honestly, the trick is to add a hand full of chopped dates when cooking the curry, you're welcome). She would joke it was all just a ploy to entice her into veganism, again, she wasn't wrong, we tried our best.

I've sketched her a few times, I even sketched her once on stage, it was an absolute failure, but a good lesson on how sometimes it's better to capture someone's energy or essence rather than to go for an accurate depiction. I framed those sketches and donated them to a fund raiser when she was going through chemo and the community that loved her was rallying around to try to help. I really wanted to sketch her again before she died, but regretfully I never found the chance, or the right words to approach that topic. Her long-term partner Nicola is an amazing photographer and she nailed Candy's attitude and struggles a few times in a few photographic portraits, so I felt like I had no real reason to step in. I really wish I had tried though, lesson learnt there.

At her memorial, she was described as many incredible things such as a warrior or a visionary, these seemed accurate enough, she was also described by a few of the speakers as fearless. While I want to remember my friend warmly and with the comfort of disregarding our disagreements, I unfortunately have one last argument to pick; Candy was never fearless, I have seen her enough times before going on stage and she definitely felt fear. Before her Queerstories talk a few months before she passed, I gave her a hug and I felt her body shaking with nerves. I say this not to draw attention to any weakness, but to emphasise her naturalness, her realness. Her strengths, her determination and power were only a small element of her and I think we do her a disservice by only partially portraying her powers now she is gone. Yes, Candy Royalle on stage was a visionary and yes, she was an absolute warrior, fuck, she was a powerhouse of passion, but she was also human and fallible and authentic and flawed and she worked really hard at keeping herself real.

I lose my friend twice if first I lose her first to cancer and then also to a misrepresentation.

To me, she will always have my respect and love. I know, as someone with a public platform, when we have a voice that will be heard in public, we have to be very vigilant about what we choose to say. We have to make difficult choices constantly about who we present as and choose to be, whilst visible on those platforms. Candy always presented as strong and invincible, and she mostly was, but she was never only those things.

There is an incredible bravery to feeling fear and still speaking up regardless, and in that I think that is where Candy's true strength lay; she wasn't fearless, she was incredibly brave.

Let's leave the empty sound bites to the toothy teenagers on social media. I saw Candy over many years transform into someone who was driven by passion and authenticity, by realness and genuineness, and I know how hard it is to do that, certainly to have done it publicly is beautifully commendable.

I was lucky to see firsthand the hard and sometimes probably terrifying work that went into Candy living her best life, yet relentlessly she chose to do it and to stick authentically to her path right up till the very end, which to me is the genuine definition of living our best life.

BECOMING AWARE OF APPROACHING FOOTSTEPS

BECOMING AWARE OF APPROACHING FOOTSTEPS

Some paintings just have to be painted. They play around in my head relentlessly like a catchy pop song and although I sometimes struggle keeping them motivated and nourished until they are ready to be brought into the world, I ultimately know they will come into being at some point in some form.

One of the memories of my youth, specifically my teen years and early twenties, is not of an event or particular experience, but of a feeling. It was a ubiquitous dreadful and dark feeling of always needing to be alert, of always keeping an eye over my shoulder.

From a very young age I was always quite obviously gay, not exactly stereotypically camp-type-gay, but I was always a little too flamboyant and arty, or as younguns say nowadays, I was 'extra'.

Sadly as a result of this, I would often find myself the target of unwanted attention or, even worse, actual violent, physical attack. I grew up in a very working class and rural area in the North East of England and quite honestly, they were simply not ready for, or appreciative of, my particular type of fabulousness.

Verbal abuse, being spat at, ripped clothing … I have a good few memories of specific incidents of unprepared-for violence, both at school and in the years afterwards travelling to and from fashion college.

I thought the random assaults would stop once I moved to London in the New Romantic late eighties (with arguably the trashiest but best fashion and music ever in the history of the world) but if anything, the unwanted attention and hostility from the straight world increased along with my own sense of daring, fashion choices and splendour-on-a-budget.

What would any of us do in such circumstances? We either let those oppressors weigh down our wings with their judgements or we climb their dull prejudices, like steps, for a clearer launch to fly.

Fast forward a few decades to now and that feeling of mild internalised panic and/or constant alertness has subsided considerably, and that combined with better understanding of how to 'pass' or how to go unnoticed, means I feel a lot more at ease in communal spaces and public transport. (Also, it's worth pointing out, fashion now, *pfft*, honestly, where are the fucking risks? Where's the platform shoes, the men in skirts, the ruffle shirts?) Anyway, that's not to say I don't still occasionally feel the odd tingle of dread, when, for example, I'll walk into some straight bar in a rural area. Special-ness is like glitter, you'll never truly get rid of it all no matter how hard life scrubs at it.

Specifically, that memory, that feeling of being weighted down, that dread; that's what this painting is about.

It is about the unfair cost of having the bravery to go out into the world, fully knowing you are displaying, what some would consider, a challenging amount of fabulousness, and there's a good chance your clothing will be pulled at, your appearance laughed at, your face spat into, or a curse, a punch, or a kick aimed your way for daring to be different.

But you know, some boys like boys, some girls like girls and some people can't wear beige or sweatpants, so get over it!

Violence is never the answer, but it can sometimes stop the questions. I remember as a teenage baby-gay, back in the rough streets of North East England, seeing a group of 'lads' hassle a drag queen; they stupidly verbally abused her and then started shoving her around. There were about four or five of them and they were obviously very safe in that number with their shields of unthought-through masculinity. Clearly none of them had ever worn stilettoes and understood the sheer lethal strength of those things. I wonder if the fella who got spiked in the face by the sharp end of the drag queens' shoe, as she wielded it with ninja style swiftness and force, ever realised he brought that upon himself. She understandably attacked in self-defence, and by the gang's intention someone was going to leave that space bleeding, and someone did, however not all of us pushed around by groups of lads have such formidable fierceness or ability to send our attackers running.

The Sydney-based and utterly inspiring performance artist Mara Maya Devi and I talked a lot about this painting before they sat for me. Although I had had this painting in my head for so long, it was a very familiar melody to me. And I needed to know that the message behind it was a shared experience and something that we both understood. Mara is 'everything' (now, I know for a fact young people say that ALL the time!) and they (Mara's pronouns are they and them) are fabulous in ways that I wish I was and always wanted to be. But just like me, half a world away and many decades ago, the world is unfortunately still not always ready for Mara's magnificent, fabulous bravery and yes, they modelled that feeling for me, very easily and knowingly.

The painting is called 'Becoming aware of approaching footsteps' and is a representation of that particular sinking feeling in the gut, that most of the LGBTQI community (and women and people of colour) know only too well.

Who is approaching, what is their intention? Friend or foe? Armed or unarmed?

It is a portrait, of Mara, yes, but also a portrait of that split second before fear kicks in, when, with a heavy heart and resigned stiffening you realise once more, that the world still might not be ready for your kind of fabulous.

It saddens me that all these decades after my youth, when this painting first appeared in my head, it can still find meaning in the world. I can only hope when Mara gets to my age, this painting and this feeling of dread has no resonance with anyone anymore and is nothing but a long-gone memory, like some trashy 80s pop song no-one remembers.

SOME ANIMALS ARE MORE EQUAL THAN OTHERS

SOME ANIMALS ARE MORE EQUAL THAN OTHERS

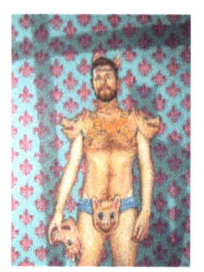 I met Andrew Batt-Rawden for the first time when I was sketching him. He and I were featured in a (really bad, predictably salacious) newspaper article about nudity and performance art and I reached out to see if he would be interested in working together. His self-assurance was stunning, he literally met me, shook hands, stripped naked and confidently chatted the entire time. It's worth pointing out at the time we were in my studio, as opposed to, let's say, a bus stop or supermarket, although knowing Andrew, he'd be completely fine bare ass naked in those situations also! And of course why wouldn't he be confident, he is ridiculously good looking, tall, fit, educated and also very talented. He is the kind of man I always thought I wanted to be, but realistically there is so much more to his story than the external and the obvious.

It's such a cliché to say when you meet someone you have no idea what demons they are battling, but it's true.

I worked with Andrew multiple times after that on a few different creative projects. Along with his confidence came an openness about a history of physical and sexual abuse that left him emotionally scarred and, like myself, an adult life of processing exactly what the hell had happened to us as children. I was lucky (well kind of), I only had to face the two-headed demon of mental and physical abuse; Andrew was dealing with those and also sexual abuse. I suppose the very simple message I'm trying to share is, the portrait you see here, on first glance, is very shiny, bright and colourful, not to mention sexually confident, but we all need to train ourselves to see not just those exteriors, but to look beyond that. I like this portrait of Andrew because it shows openly his darker side and his consciously developed 'sex pig' persona that he uses in his performance art practice.

I could waffle on at this point about the meaning of the various elements of the painting (the shadow of the cross for example) but you know what, nah, I'm just going to say, let's just all try to be kind to one another because I'm still yet to meet somebody in this world who doesn't have at least a little bit of trauma to work though and life is short and so am I. Be kind.

MUCH FREEDOM

MUCH FREEDOM

 I just got home from seeing a friend's exhibition.

It was a good show, but it left me feeling a bit icky.

I think he's being really exploited and, other than just trying to be a supportive friend, I don't really think there's anything I can do about it.

His work is really good. I won't describe it too much, because I think it's unfair to single him out and make it obvious to anyone who knows him; but I think the stuff he does comes from a deep dark place inside of him and there is a price to pay for that deep mining (and I'm not just referring to the ridiculously high percentage of all sales the gallery takes). And I fear it's unsustainable mining. He really pours his heart onto his canvases through exploration around isolation and trauma. I just don't feel that's a good thing in this instance. I think he might be destroying any chance of happiness, and connecting with the world, one exhibition at a time. He seems so tired and jaded.

Creative souls are often sensitive souls and we need extra time to heal from our wounds and battles.

And sometimes, reliving the battle to depict that on canvas only succeeds in reopening the wounds we need to let heal. The gallery system here in Sydney can be quite 'bleed them till they're dry or dying' kinda thing, and I try to have as little to do with it as I can. In fairness it's worth pointing out that since I never actually studied art and don't play the 'wanky art game' the gallery system in Sydney also wants very little to do with me. I like the Groucho Marx quote, 'I would never want to join any club that would accept me as a member'.

Galleries rarely value the artists; they value the money the artists can make for the gallery owners. In my experience, that's generally it.

Years ago, in London when I was in my early twenties, a tad firmer and a lot more fuckable, I dabbled in sex work. I say dabbled, because like most things I tried at that age, I was rather uncommitted and a tad vague, so I can't really claim to have chosen it as a profession or calling.

I had a good friend who was with an 'escort agency' in Earl's Court. He would sit in the shockingly-lit living room of a rather ordinary terrace house and gentlemen would come in and peer at him and a few other young men (it's worth stressing they were all above legal age, but maturity wise, often very much still boys) through something that looked very much like a confessional grate wedged into the serving hatch between the old kitchen which had been badly converted into a bar. The customers would then pick out their favorite fella, take them upstairs and pay on the way out for whatever services they accumulated.

I would often go and collect my friend before a night out partying, or sometimes meet him for drinks/shots/a toke of a joint on his 'lunch break' (around midnight) and I made friends with a few of his coworkers, so it kind of happened organically, that I too, would end up taking a seat in that suburban sitting room of sin.

I was fine with doing sex work. As someone who grew up constantly shamed for my sexuality, I'd given up expecting or needing approval for my choices around it.

However, out of all the jobs I've ever done, I was probably the worst at this by far. I'd do everything I wasn't supposed to (ask way too many personal questions, challenge what I was being asked to do, concern myself far more with my orgasm than theirs) and do nothing that I was supposed to (such as be discreet: yeah, you can have my personal number, of course I'd love to go on a date, let's not tell anyone we did that and you can have that for free because I rather enjoyed it too!). I didn't last long, I was obviously a bit of a liability, although it did lead to my next job as operator on a telephone sex line. Now that was fun.

It was back in the day before mobiles so people (men) would ring up from their landlines and pay a premium rate per minute to chat to, well, *whoever* they wanted really. I created a number of characters with a selection of accents. Because I was unseen by the caller, I could be younger, older, Northern, Cockney, tall, blonde, dark, posh tottie, innocent ingénue or a rough and randy tradie; whatever was needed. I would often put a caller on hold while I *went to fetch another phone operator*, which was basically me doing a different voice. It was a ridiculous amount of fun.

Although the hours cut into my social life, I actually really liked it, the pay was okay and I made full use of the mute button to collapse into hysterics many times per shift. There was a very mixed bag of us working there, but all of us used humour and a cheeky camaraderie to get through. The trick was to get the callers to a point of not being able to hang up, but not exactly ready to cum because once they did, they'd hang up, and end of call meant end of cashola.

Maybe in hindsight the management of the Escort Agency putting me forward for a telephone job with a different company wasn't the biggest compliment ever, a little like being told you have the perfect face for radio; but it took me out of the world of paid sex work before I became jaded, so I suppose that is a good thing. The same telephone company

ran premium rate lines where you could call up and listen to a story rather than talk to a real live (although, in my case, lying-through-their-teeth) operator. I recorded a fair few of these stories and then progressed to also writing them. I was Pete the frisky plumber, here to give your pipes a right good cleaning out. I was Jeremy the strict Naval Officer and you have been a naughty, naughty cadet. I was Beverly the cross-dressing dentist who couldn't wait to get you into her chair with your head back. And so on and so forth. Ooh the filth, ooh the fun! (It's funny to think these recordings probably still exist somewhere in the world, I can't wait for them to come back and haunt me at some point!)

I got to play with identity and sexuality within the safety of anonymity, and it was the perfect playground for me to decide who I wanted to be and to learn a little bit more about life.

I relate all of this to my friend who just had the exhibition because this was the time when I first really realised we are all a commodity, we can all be exploited. It all comes down to what we are prepared, and able, to offer the world. Just like people can adore you, build you up and worship you, people can also let you down, bully you and eat at your self-esteem if you let them.

Did I tell my friends at the time about these jobs? You bet your knickers I did; I dined out on these stories for years afterwards! However, did I tell my dad about those blow-jobbing-jobs? Nope. I was still susceptible to shame, hence not telling my old man about my chosen route of employment, but other than that, in my own mind, I really didn't, and don't, feel ashamed of that period of my life at all.

I only sat in that room in Earls Court a few times over a few weeks and I only worked 'on the lines' for a little over a year, but both jobs served me well and I paid my taxes. I'm a big believer in how sex work can (although not in every instance) empower those who are able to look after themselves.

It's when others look at you and only see dollar signs or a pound of flesh to be exploited that problems arise.

I see so many parallels between sex work and art work. Both can offer glamour and excitement if that's what you are looking for, but both will chew you up and spit you out if you can't stand up for yourself or don't have the confidence to say no.

Both avenues of employment depend on potential and the commodification or exploitation of that potential. I think it comes down to how much we, the willing participant (and what I'm talking about here is a best-case scenario, we are willing) are prepared to trade on our potential. Whether it's creativity or cunnilingus, when cash is involved a price can be popped on either.

Is my friend being exploited by this gallery? Yeah, absolutely.

Is he being bum-fucked for money? Yeah, kinda.

Will he recover? Yeah, hopefully.

Will it leave him jaded enough to permanently harm his creative output? Yeah, probably.

Do I wish it were different? Fuck yeah.

The image of the bikes that goes with this written piece is connected vaguely in as much as it is about freedom. We are all different, we all have different life experiences and we all make up a big and complex picture.

Some of us chose our path; some of us don't have that privilege. Let's not judge each other.

My father passed away when I was in my mid-thirties. At that point I would have been willing to open the conversation with him about what I talk about in the previous pages. However once he got his cancer diagnosis anything like that was understandably off the table, so it never happened, well, that and the fact we lived in different hemispheres and this was in a day before Facetime.

The very last conversation that I had with him, on the phone, the day before I flew from Australia to see him in hospital, back in the UK, he said more than anything he wanted me to be happy. Unfortunately he also said he wanted me to not be gay and find 'good woman'. That was the very last time we spoke and I hurried him off the phone for fear of what else he might say. When I got to London my ex-boyfriend picked me up from the airport and told me my father had died a few hours before. Typical of the fucker not to give me a final goodbye.

I've found many a good woman, but none of them made me not want to be gay, in fact I found many a good man that confirmed quite the opposite. I wish I'd been able to talk to Dad more about things, but hey. He passed away not knowing a lot of things about his son, and maybe he wanted that, I don't know, but either way, it makes me sad that we never had that kind of honesty or acceptance.

I'll try to talk to my friend about leaving his gallery and becoming more independent as an artist. It'll be a challenging conversation because he's very caught up in the pretentiousness of the art scene that he's in. But you know, for the sake of our friendship, I have to try. Maybe I could make the conversation more fun by slipping into character and bringing back Larry the lusty Lollipop man …

AT HER MOST APPROACHABLE

AT HER MOST APPROACHABLE

 This is a painting of my friend Michelle Frances Collocott. It is one of many paintings I've done of her. She is a painter whose work I really admire. I also admire her. She is a trans woman who transitioned back when it wasn't as (relatively) easy as it is now.

She and I first met when I was working in an art supply store and she came in with her dog Freddie looking for a specific archival coloured tissue. She was a bit grumpy and a bit shy and didn't want to chat but we didn't have the yellow archival tissue paper she was looking for, so she had to tell me what type she wanted so we could order some. Long story short, I was a bit shit at my job and never ordered her any tissue, but she kept coming in to check on the progress of her order, so we got to know each other, and our friendship blossomed. I don't think I ever got around to telling her I didn't put the order through, so when she reads this she'll probably be all grumpy with me again. Oops.

Michelle never liked this painting. I kind of understood why not. It isn't my best. And isn't even my best of her. I wanted to portray her as I saw her at that point in our friendship; gradually opening up and warming to the viewer, but not completely relaxed or completely trusting.

People always ask about the recurring motive in the background of my paintings; the fleur de lis.

They often ask as if there would be a simple easy answer, but there isn't. I like the recurring pattern for many reasons and those reasons often change in order of relevance.

I incorporate it into most of my portraits mainly because of the idea of 'false flags' and what that represents. I think we live in a time where we are sold a lot of bullshit and a lot of what we strive for in life is actually really quite worthless. Rarely things are what they seem. Fake news (oh god I hate that expression). Many years ago I was told that the fleur de lis was the standard (flag) used by the French when they were at war with the English. The idea was that the standard bearers would be fiercely protected and forge their way forward through the field of battle so the following French armies could always look up and would know which direction to fight in and gain ground. The English worked this out and made false standards of their own to purposely confuse the French and draw them back, fighting into the direction from which they came. A brilliant and destructive idea which appeals to both my sense of humour and frustrations at the modern world. However, I once enthusiastically spoke about this theory with a historian (of course I did because I'm an idiot) who basically shot down the whole idea and laughed at my lack of research. Damn, well don't I look like a fool. But if anything, that actually just made me connect with that pointy little motif more! Brilliant, a false flag wrapped up in another nonsensical false flag! I also like the idea that a lot of people connect the image of the fleur de lis with affluence, modern branding and wealth, (yuk) which I'm happy to meddle and headfuck with, because if you aspire to that nonsense you deserve to have that challenged. I also like it because of the appearance of working-class domestic wallpaper, the idea that the queer and fabulous creatures I portray could just be sitting at home, casually looking as drop dead gorgeous as they do.

Michelle is the opposite of me, she studied art and even went on to teach painting at one of the best art schools in Australia. She knows her shit and does loads of research for her work and can name artists I've never heard of. Girl got the clevers. Anyway, Michelle never did get her tissue but she did get a good friend who loves her to bits.

A PERFECT EXAMPLE OF TRADITIONAL PORTRAITURE

AS SEEN THROUGH THE EYES OF A TRADITIONALLY BROUGHT UP WESTERNER

A PERFECT EXAMPLE OF TRADITIONAL PORTRAITURE

AS SEEN THROUGH THE EYES OF A TRADITIONALLY BROUGHT UP WESTERNER

Privilege is a funny old thing. Please allow me to sketch a simple representation out for you (as I see it) in basic tones with a bit of crosshatching for dramatic effect. The comfortable, sundrenched top rung on the ladder of privilege is where cis, white, abled-bodied, educated, employed men sit. The rungs nearer the damp and well-shaded bottom of the ladder are where, for example, a trans female, same-sex-attracted, disabled, refugee of colour are expected (or forced) to sit. Now, how you see the order of the rungs (and indeed, how many rungs there are) in between the top and bottom, would vary depending on who you are and how you get to experience the world, but you get the general picture I'm sketching for you here.

Society undoubtedly places you somewhere on that ladder, whether you want to be there or not. The problem is that the rewards are all at the top (where a lot of people are just majestically placed at birth) and those at the bottom are not given a fair chance to climb or reap life's rewards. Please do take a moment to picture this (somewhat clumsy) portrayal.

I am both cursed and blessed when it comes to privilege, although who am I kidding, certainly more blessed. I'm white (tick), I'm male-bodied (tick), I'm able-bodied (tick). The list of my DNA-given-glories goes on, but there's also a few struggles thrown in there to complicate things. I certainly do not have a high income (however, obviously, if you've ever seen me in swimwear you'll know, I clearly never go without food). I'm an immigrant in the country I live in (although, come on, I'm the same skin colour as the colonisers of that country and my immigration was my own choice, so really my struggle is minimal in comparison to other immigrants). I'm a femme (ish) queer who chooses to make his living in the creative world, but never completed further education (which means I never actually studied art, so realistically there's little chance I will ever really be taken seriously as an artist, but that I could even try, speaks volumes about privileges offered to me). Basically I'm not sitting on the top rung of the ladder swinging my legs looking down, but from where I am, I get to feel sunlight on my face and enjoy a good view!

The negatives in my life are vastly, vastly outweighed by the positives, I'm the first to admit; but as I said, privilege is a funny old thing and the ladder of privilege can sometimes be a winding and wiggly one with a few surprise turns and slippery steps.

Oppression is a funny old thing, too, although, hmm, actually, obviously really isn't. Ever. Oppression is both my nemesis and my inspiration. It fights me and fuels me. I vow to use all I have to vanquish it, yet I call upon it often to fill my creative sails and push me forward with a power I am yet to find elsewhere. Oppression is like a big solid turd that I roll in golden glitter and slice beautifully to make medals for myself out of

(although, not really … please tell me you do know I don't really do that, don't you?)

Without doubt I have suffered from oppression, but I constantly meet others who make my tales of oppression and struggle seem like a picnic on a sunny day, fully catered for and fully licenced. I get it, I get to enjoy a quality view from the height I have been placed on life's ladder, yet my own (albeit micro) oppression feels no less real and debilitating to me. Those oppressions are no less real than house bricks dropped in my pockets from above, weighing me down to keep me in my place.

In my art practise I struggle constantly with knowing where the line sits between exploitation and representation. How can I tell when my wish to represent, and elevate, diversity starts to infringe on the artistic no-no of cultural appropriation? A very primary part of my work is to use my skill and platform to elevate the profile and social standing of under-represented minorities, whether that be queer people, people of colour, the differently abled, people who identify themselves as being on the spectrum of neuro diversity, the list goes on. It's all about the un-other-ising of the underdog, I try to lift them (us) up a little using the supposed grandiosity of traditional portraiture that civilised society respects and reveres. It is well within my skill set and social standing to do so, it is little hardship to me. But what I struggle with and what others are often only too happy to point out is, are these stories I depict mine to tell?

Honestly, it fucks with my mind. I try to never exploit, but how can I represent and portray without a little of that sneaking in? At what point does what I do become the exploitation of others for my own creative gain? I can only try my best as part of the artistic composition of any piece to know where to place that particular line.

I tell you, it's an absolute total and utter fucking minefield and it can stifle my creative process like nothing else. Would you like a side-serving of self-analysis paralysis with that creative urge? The people I'm drawn to paint are normally those with a tale to tell and a few of life's poo medals pinned to their chests (pinned there by themselves or by others), but yet I beat myself up constantly debating in my head whether or not I am using my powers for good, or the total opposite of everything good: really bad art.

Shahmen (or pictured here as their fabulous, creative and elegant alias, Radha La Bia) is a gorgeous soul I'd see out and about at various arty events in Sydney and they were always very approachable, fun and cheeky. I know them only vaguely in a queer arty community kinda way, but to me, it seems they have forged the frustrations and oppressions that life has no doubt thrown at them, into a glorious and fabulous identity. I'm sure there is more than that to Shahmen's story, but that is not my story to tell, not mine.

There's a stumbling block I often have to get around when I decide I want someone to sit for me and that's plucking up the courage to ask them. It's so utterly ridiculous. I've won awards, I've won art prizes and have regular exhibitions. I'm an artist for god's sake! Yet I still feel like such a loser-wannabe when it comes to actually saying those words, 'Will you please sit for me?' It's nerve wracking and I have yet to formularise a way of doing it where I don't look like an absolute eejiot.

I'm kind of (mostly) happy with the outcome, I really like the frame (although *I* can say that, *you* are NEVER allowed to say that to an artist, it's the worst, worst, worst insult ever!). I had so many visions of how I wanted to paint Shahmen. I wanted them in a much more elaborate and luxurious setting, with more drapery, rich colours and textures but I downsized on that vision because I couldn't work out where the line between objectifying their cultural background and depicting their ownership of their cultural background sat. I also stumbled on that conversation with Shahmen. Stupid me. My white privilege hindered me, my fear of cultural appropriation tripped me and lacking the life experiences to think my way through it all, I buckled somewhat and just middle-grounded it. I debilitated myself with more strength than any outside force ever has.

Anyway, so back to that pesky ladder, my point is, if we aren't somehow using our strengths and abilities to support and encourage others on the rungs (that society has deemed) below us to climb up, then what are we doing? If we are blocking the accent of others then we are part of the problem. Yes, those above us may be (tactically) standing on our fingers, but we can still let others climb over us or pass though us if need be. I actively try to do this, it's difficult, it's messy and it's unknown territory that colonial life hasn't prepared me for, but I try. Let's turn this motherfucking ladder upside down and let's share that sunshine.

TWELVE PEOPLE WHO WILL NEVER SIT DOWN NEXT TO ME AGAIN

TWELVE PEOPLE WHO WILL NEVER SIT DOWN NEXT TO ME AGAIN

As well as having a slight obsession with painting bikes, it seems I can't really help myself when it comes to chairs also.

And again, it comes down to portraying a space for potential and a sense of being. I think the title of this one kind of explains what the piece is about.

I'm not very good at dealing with grief, I mean I suppose none of us are when it comes down to it. After I moved to London my first proper boyfriend took his own life when he was 21. I was a year or two younger and to say it fucked me up is an understatement. At the time, however, I put a lot of effort into blocking out the trauma of it all. Since he'd 'heartlessly' broken up with me a few months before he died I felt like I had no real right to claim grief, and since he'd pushed me away first, I, in return, pushed away everything I felt at his passing. The potential lost with him is ridiculous. He was utterly brilliant and the world was just beginning to open up for him.

He had found out he was HIV-positive and, added into other struggles he was facing, it all got too much I suppose. He and I had unprotected sex before his diagnosis and, for the next few years following his passing, I

chose to remain untested, just believing I too would be HIV-positive, but unable to cope with any proper confirmation. Anyway, turns out I wasn't, but I stupidly still went through the trauma and head fuck of thinking I was. Typical me. Typically stupid. I like to think I've changed since then, but I'm clever enough to know I'm probably still really quite stupid.

Anyway, grief, it does horrible things to your brain, your self-esteem and any possible potential you may have and in my early twenties I also had to also deal with my mum passing and then my grandmother and then, well, the list goes on, blah blah. Life can be shit, grief is shit, but the alternative is much shittier still. The lucky ones are the ones who get to live through it all.

The colours in this piece are of dried blood and of parchment, representing death and memory. It is about the loss of potential but also just about loss on its own. It's in the shape of a cross although grief hangs us all up and crucifies us all regardless of whatever belief system gives us faith.

The point I'm trying to make though is appreciate the time you have, the people you have around you, the health you have and the ability to be present and in your own life. Who the fuck knows what happens next? We all leave an empty seat at some point.

FROM A SPARK TO A FLAME

FROM A SPARK
TO A FLAME

 I have one of those funny creative minds.
When people say certain words
I often unintentionally envisage that word as a
colour or shape; when I stare at people I'm
often working out what it is that makes their
face uniquely and recognisably theirs;
and when I stare vaguely off into the distance there's a very good chance
I'll be thinking about perspective and working out the degrees from the
horizon needed to map out a convincing vanishing point. Oh yes, I have
a strange and creative mind.

Whenever I hear anyone say out-loud the acronym LGBTQI(+A) I
usually and unfortunately, in my mind, picture those little foam toe
separator things that people use when doing nail varnish or getting a
pedicure, you know the ones.

The reason these funny foam toe separator things come to mind (usually
they are pink or purple, aren't they, I wonder why that is …) is because
the singular letters L.G.B.T.Q.I. (+A) always seem like such separate
entities; part of a big thing, yes, but different parts of a thing; different
protrusions from a shared starting point. Like, yeah, us peeps on
that acronym spectrum are all joined by the experience
of being the repressed underdogs of society, sure, but I'm pretty

damn certain someone finding their way in the world as intersex has a very different set of challenges than say, someone who has just come out as a lesbian.

I love the idea of the camaraderie shared by the communities unified by the umbrella term LGBTQI+A, but then I also wish we didn't even have need for that term. Labels are for jam-jars, Tupperware lids, boxes of sex toys when you move house to make sure you freak out the removalists, and for things kept under sinks that small children shouldn't drink.

This is a painting of my friend Felicity, she performs spoken word burlesque (now there we are, that's another under-represented minority right there!) under the evocative (and to be honest, a tad camp) stage name Ember Flame. I first met Felicity over a decade ago, when she was shy and wore very thick lensed glasses, she was very beautiful, but everybody else knew that more than she did. Felicity is a lot more aware of her beauty and abilities now. She is also a lot more confident and, I believe, happier in herself. I certainly wouldn't have expected her to be confident to pose naked for me when I first met her; confidence can lead to confidence, I suppose, and in her case I'm so lucky to have been witness to that voyage of development and awakening.

Felicity's best friend at school was a lesbian and they are still indisputable, inseparable besties, Felicity's (very, very) favourite fellow in the world happens to be my (very, very) gay boyfriend and she's probably very nearly drunkenly danced in just as many gay clubs as I have. In my mind, I would definitely class Felicity as queer. She's like so aesthetically queer, imaginative and very left of centre, yet she is also a heterosexual cis woman who likes a bit of peen. So how does this work in the bumpy pink toe-separator of the big long acronym? Technically Felicity is a +A on the LGBTQI(+A) spectrum. She is an ally. My next exhibition is exclusively celebrating people like Felicity, it is called '+A (plus Allies)' and it is a celebration of individuals who don't necessarily pop the bits of somebody of the same sex as them into their orifices on a recurring basis, but they are people who are wholly supportive, encouraging and positively connected to the LGBTQI world.

For the past few years, here in Australia, ooh, we've certainly needed our allies and bless their little straight hearts, some of those awesome people have delivered in spades! I've made quite a bit of a name for myself in the past with rather vibrant and boldly coloured portraits of LGBTQI individuals, but this coming exhibition, over Sydney's Mardi Gras festival, is to rejoice in those beautiful souls that wouldn't normally get a proper mention in the acronym until the very end.

The exhibition is on at the ridiculously heterosexual venue of the Bondi Pavilion, overlooking Bondi Beach. I'm starting with an empty gallery and will be sketching and painting people who wander past, step forward and identify themselves as allies. Look, I'll be honest, I'm expecting mixed results, probably lots of hugs, tears and new-best-friends-forever on my part, but also a few 'quite interesting' conversations with people who don't align themselves with my beliefs, which I am completely up for (although also dreading a bit, because I hate confrontation and I fear there may be a little bit of attitude from those not wholeheartedly on the same page as me when it comes to uniting communities).

My secret weapon in these conversations is creative projects create creative mindsets, believe me, it's true, I'm staking my professional reputation on it!

The ulterior motive of this exhibition is to rid my mind of those weird toe separator things when LGBTQI(+A) people are mentioned. I don't want separate protruding bits coming out of our communities or any communities; I want the gaps in those yukky sponge things filled with wonderful friends and allies, I want everyone to be an ally to everyone, indeed at some point in life everyone needs an ally of some sort. I want smooth, gap free, level playing fields and nothing that looks like a speed bump on our road to equality, as we, all of us, regardless of sexuality, support each other as one. When I think of humankind, instead of some peoples 'isms' being on a simple spectrum, I want to picture a beautiful multi coloured sphere, like the most spectacular beach ball ever inflated. Pulsating like a heartbeat, one that is formed from within, but also happens to shape the external world that it comes into contact with, colouring it with sound, strength, humour, acceptance, creativity, compassion and, most of all, love, as it spins into infinity.

I mean come on, as far-fetched as that image may be, surely that's a far more appealing visual than one of those weird little foam toe separators!

UNFINISHED

UNFINISHED

I always finish paintings. Even if I lose interest in them, I always finish them.

This is pretty much the only painting I have ever really undertaken where I haven't (yet) finished it. It's sat in its current state in my studio for the past 2 years. It is my friend Mai, and she is super-inspiring and super-awesome.

I remember starting this painting and wanting to say something about the outdated ridiculousness of 'gender appropriate clothing' but somewhere along the way I just got derailed/lost/confuselled/who the hell knows.

I don't even (yet) have a final title for it; I did think about calling it either 'What you looking at?' or, 'Mai was always fun to go shoe shopping with', but thought better of both of those. Suggestions on a postcard please.

I'm not even 100% sure why I painted in all of the shoes! It took me a couple of days and I painted them in on such a whim. What are they saying? What do they mean? Was I possessed by some sort of psychotic sling-back-suggesting shoe demon? Obviously, all those shoes probably meant something on the day I painted them, but I have zero idea what exactly that could be now!

I think the pivotal point of this piece being finished is what I paint in the reflection of the mirror. Who to paint in, who to paint in … Mai has four children and I was thinking about painting them, but it might be a bit squishy. I will put some time aside at some point and finish it. I really have to, guilt will guide my hand on that.

Maybe more shoes?

No! No more shoes!

Gawd bless her! Mai sat in my front room baring her breasts long enough for me, so I definitely have to do something with it.

I don't *not* connect to it as it is, though; it definitely makes a statement, I'm just not sure exactly what it says anymore, and I just don't think it looks quite complete (yet). I suppose the lesson here is: know what you're saying before you start saying it; although as we all know, where's the fun in that?

Maybe more shoes …

SIGNS OF A STRUGGLE

SIGNS OF A STRUGGLE

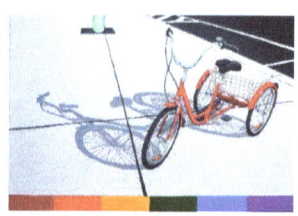

So now you've seen inside my imagination and you've also read my thoughts.

What more can I tell you? I hope I make all of this look easy because, most of the time it is. Easy to me and essential to me. You too should paint, or draw, or write, or create in some way if you don't already. I suppose that's my takeaway message from all of this: be more creative. Represent your thoughts. Even if it's just with glittery eyeshadow on a cloudy Tuesday morning or a more extravagant recipe for a Thursday evening's dinner; get creative, why the fuck not.

If you dabble in 'the arts' already or if this encourages you to start, I doubt you'll have the same style as me, the same hand, or the same things to say, but somewhere within you there is a story, or vision, or a view, to share with the world. Archive your existence creatively in some way, but also don't care who sees it or worry about what they might think.

I've called this collection of writings/pictures/works Signs Of A Struggle, because really, that's what they all are. Most days I win, some days I don't, but the struggle is real, by reading this you've shared the struggle with me. I co-run a fortnightly drawing group here in Sydney called LOVElines for older LGBTQI people and everyone, without fail has some kind of struggle, issue or experience that benefits from being put through a creative thought process.

Being creative has literally saved my life. It has given me a bridge to the outside world countless times. If I wasn't creative god knows what state (or maximum security hospital) I would be in. It stands to reason the only thing that would guide me out of darkness would be colour and light. I get grumpy and impossible to be around if I haven't sketched, painted or written anything for a while. It's sad, but true, Ryan, my partner, has had to struggle his way through many an overdramatic man-strop from me because all I need to do is sit and sketch and calm my mind and I can't find time to fit it into my week.

The reason I decided to finish on this piece is not just because of what the subject matter is but because of the backstory.

It was a bike outside a cycle hire shop just beside where Ryan's parents live in rural New South Wales. I was walking with him and his parents and I stopped to stare at the bike, but rather marvellously they didn't stop to stare at me; they just accepted I'd seen something that interested me and they just kept walking and talking, as if my whims and oddities are nothing to be bothered by.

I liked the composition of this bike for a few reasons; I liked that this odd little tricycle, unusual in its design, stood proudly out on its own, undeterred by the world around it. Just doing its own thing, being just what it was, nothing special really, but with unlimited potential for possible journeys.

That's all.

It seems fitting to end with a bike painting as I peddle off on my merry way.

Thank you for reading.

Guy James Whitworth, October 2019

ACKNOWLEDGEMENTS

A big thank you to …

Ryan the most lovable car farter in the world.

Gordon for being a reet canny lad, a brilliant editor, and for making this book happen.

My sisters, you all shaped me and we are all just bits of each other at different times. Sorry I keep missing your birthdays.

All of the models who sat for me. In these and countless other paintings, it is actually true, without you (all) I am nothing. Thank you for the inspiration and for the sitting still and listening to me talk nonsense.

To my friends who inspire, tolerate and mock me, Lady B, Roger Craig, A la Carter, I deserve the mocking and you all keep me both amused, alert and humble.

www.ingramcontent.com/pod-product-compliance
Lightning Source LLC
Chambersburg PA
CBHW041606240626
47164CB00009B/195